Party Planning Hel Favors, Food, Invites, and More Ideas for a Successful Party

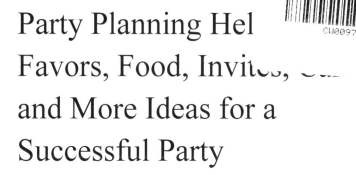

Table of Contents

Party Supplies Needed: 5

Party Planning Checklist 6

Tips For Planning A Party 8

    Invitations 8

    Decorations 9

    Food 9

    Music 10

How to Choose a Theme for Your Party 11

    Things You Should Consider 11

        Type of Crowd- 11

        Budget- 11

        Occasion- 11

        Children's Party Themes 12

        Adult Party Themes 13

How to Plan a Surprise Party 14

    Setting a Date 14

    Making the Guest List 14

    Keeping the Secret 15

    Getting Your Guest of Honor to the Party 15

    Surprise! 16

Create Birthday Party Decorations Cheaply 17

    Shop Wisely 17

    Table Decor 17

    Party Decor 18

    Banners and Hanging Decorations 18

    Decorating the Cake 19

    Decorating the Outdoors 19

Ideas for Making Your Own Party Invitations 20

    Invitations for Youngsters 20

Invitations for Older Children 20

Invitations for Teenagers 21

Outdoor Party Games 22

Sidewalk Chalk Games.. 22

Water Games 22

Traditional Games 23

Children Party Game Ideas.. 24

Simple Games... 24

Games for Older Children 26

Fun Kids Birthday Party Games Done Cheaply 28

Balloon Fun 28

Pin-the-Tail Games... 28

Pick a Duck.. 28

Musical Dress Up 29

Teenage Party Games 30

Adult-Led Fun 30

Board Games 31

Adult Party Games.. 33

Lie Detector Game.. 33

Hula Hoop Games 33

Newlywed Game 34

Message Under the Plate 34

Live Entertainment done Cheaply 36

Make your own Musical Fun 36

Puppet Playhouse Fun... 36

Silly Story in the Round Fun 37

Kids Party Crafts or Activities... 38

Toddlers and Young Children 38

Sticker Crafts and Cake Decorating... 38

Paper Crafts 38

Scavenger Hunts 39

Tips for a Perfect Baked Cake 41

Tip #1: Preparation 41

Tip #2: The Pan 41

Tip #3: Understanding the Science of Cake 42

Tip #4: Removing the Cake 42

Cake Decorating Design Ideas... 43

Simple Cake Decorating Ideas... 43

Ornate Cake Decorating 43

Elaborate Cake Decorating 44

Party Food Ideas 45

Keeping it Simple 45

BBQ Basics 45

A Fancy Tea Party 46

Just for Kids.. 46

Are You Ready for Some Football? 47

Children's Birthday Party Food.. 48

The Cake.. 48

The Menu... 48

Quick Treats 49

Tips.. 50

Party Favor Ideas and Goody Bags 51

Babies and Toddlers 51

Between Toddlers and Tweens 52

Teens.. 52

How to Sew Goodie Bags for Parties 54

Party Supplies Needed:

Theme Decorations
Balloons
Streamers
Party hats
Party horns
Confetti
Table centerpiece
Table cloth/covering
Plates and/or bowls
Silverware
Cups
Napkins
Party hats
Goody bags with party favors
Piñata and fillers
Games/ supplies needed
Party activities supplies
Cake
Party Invitations and thank you cards
Serving utensils
Candles and matches
Party food/refreshments with any utensils needed
Music
Presents

Party Planning Checklist

☺ 1 month before

Schedule date of party
Decide on a theme
Make a list of guests
Decide on location
If using party entertainment such as jumpy castles, clowns, magic shows, etc. reserve

☺ 2-3 weeks before

Prepare and send out invitations
Make a party plan for food, cake, activities and games

☺ 1-2 weeks before

Buy party decorations and supplies- see party supplies list.
Make any decorations or crafts for the party
Plan cake design
Buy presents and goody bag supplies
Bake and freeze undecorated cake.
Clean house

☺ Several days before

Buy groceries for party
Confirm games and activities that will be used for the party and make sure you have all supplies needed.

☺ 1 day before

Set up party table and decorations
Confirm number of guests
Wrap presents and goody bags
Prepare cake and decorate the night before or morning of
Prepare any food prep that can be done ahead

☺ **Day of Party**

Finish food prep

Place cake in a safe place where it can be part of the party

Set all activities and crafts ready to go

Blow up balloons

Set goodie bags by the door.

Attach balloons outside so guests know where the party house is.

Make sure bathrooms and party area are clean.

Tips For Planning A Party

Everyone will have their own tips for planning a party, but getting the right atmosphere for your own event will depend on who your guests are, what the celebration is for and your own experience of what has worked well before. As a rule, there are five things that you need to think about that can all fall under the same party theme:

Invitations
Decorations
Food
Music
Cake

One of the best tips for planning a party is to give yourself plenty of time to make these decisions, as you can always change your invitations if you suddenly get a better idea when you're planning the food, for example

Invitations

This is the first time that your guests will find out about your party, so you'll need to make sure the invitations contain all the information they'll need such as times, date, location, what they need to bring and any costumes they need to wear. Depending on the number of people coming, you can either hand make your invitations for a smaller gathering or use templates from the Internet to mass produce a lot of invites.

Of course, if it is a formal affair, you will want to have the invitations printed and sent through the mail. Lastly, be sure to use the theme of your party as a basis for the decorations on your invitations to make them fit in with the rest of the event.

Decorations

Your decorations will set the mood for your party and one of the most popular tips is to really put your effort in here to impress your guests. Your decorations w ill fall into broad categories

Tables – for a formal event, make sure that all linen is clean pressed and that you have a central floral arrangement on each table. For a family gathering, use the theme of the party to have little trinkets and objects on the table to turn the tables into a miniature landscape.

Lighting – a romantic event such as a wedding or Valentine's Day party needs soft lighting, and you can create an impressive atmosphere with just candles. For any event, try to avoid really bright lights all over as they can be better used to highlight certain features.

Walls – the walls are the canvas for your party so the best ideas are to use drapes, posters or paintings to give the walls a bit of life and turn the room into something more magical.

Food

The food that you serve is one of the most important parts of the party, and above all, you need to make sure that you're providing enough for all of your guests. You need to decide between a buffet self service and a sit down meal. If you do choose the latter, you'll need to think about how you're going to serve it, as you may need to hire staff or volunteers if there are a lot of guests.

Music

Along with the decorations, the music you choose to play will help dictate the atmosphere of your party. You can hire a DJ to run things for you if the music is a key part of the event, or for a more personalized touch you could get people to bring their favorite CDs or choose from a selection of relevant themed tracks. Either way, make sure that the music is low enough for people to be able to hear each other talk.

If you get stuck on planning your event, asking your friends and family for their tips for planning a party will give you some inspiration as well as an idea as to what things work well. You'll need to have a rough estimate of the number of guests and some theme ideas when you start asking people for their advice. Of course, the most important tip is to plan far enough in advance, that on the day of the party you can relax and enjoy yourself.

How to Choose a Theme for Your Party

Deciding how to choose a theme for your party can sometimes be difficult, especially when there are so many options from which to choose. If you are at a loss as to what kind of theme you should use, try considering what kind of celebration is it going to be. a number of factors you should consider that will help you make the best possible choice for the celebration at hand.

Things You Should Consider

Type of Crowd-

This is one of the most basic questions you must ask when learning how to choose a theme for your party. Is the party for a boy or girl? An older adult or a young child? Pinpointing exactly what individual or crowd you are looking to please will greatly increase your ability to select an appropriate theme.

Budget-

This is another factor you should consider when figuring out how to choose a theme for your party. How much money you are able to spend will have a great deal of influence over what type of party you will inevitably have. Certain themes are easier to pull off with a higher budget than others, especially those that require more details and materials. For example, an elegant, sophisticated winter wonderland themed party will almost always cost more to produce than a Tiki themed pool party.

Occasion-

It's always wise to consider the occasion when determining how to choose a theme for your party. Many types of occasions call for a celebration that is often different and unique depending on the circumstances. Is your party for a formal event like a wedding reception or prom or is it a more casual event like a birthday party or family reunion.

It is always tasteful to use a theme that reflects the event, occasion or person you are celebrating. A quinceañera, for example, is a lavish, coming of age party that is thrown for a Hispanic teenage girl when she reaches 15. This type of party is almost always a high-class, formal event.

If you were choosing a theme for this type of party, a royal princess theme may be appropriate as would a fairy tale theme because they not only reflect what the party is about but are also in line with the budget and the formal requirements.

Children's Party Themes

If you are throwing a soiree for a child, figuring out how to choose a theme for your party may not be as difficult as it may be in other situations. Children's parties, especially birthday parties are quite simple to plan as these are typically low budget events thrown to celebrate a specific child. The theme you choose for your child's birthday should be a direct reflection of his or her likes and interests. The easiest theme choices for kids can be inspired by their favorite cartoon and television characters.

A number of unconventional ideas can be used when learning how to choose a theme for your party, especially if your child's interests don't revolve around Disney princesses and television characters. Evaluate the child's goals, passions and interests to create a party theme that not everyone would think to use. Does your child have a love for pizza? Use that to create a one of a kind pizza themed party that your child will remember for years to come.

Adult Party Themes

Learning how to choose a theme for your party works just the same for adults as for children, however there is usually more planning and sophistication involved. If you are selecting a theme for an adult birthday party, consider that person's likes and interest just as you would with a child.

If you are planning an adult party that is not birthday related, like a 25th wedding anniversary for example, select a theme that reflects the people for whom the party is being held as well as the occasion. A perfect theme for a couple celebrating 25 years of marriage may be "growing old together". You could have your guests bring 'getting old' or 'over the hill' gag gifts and decorate your venue like a retirement home.

No matter what type of occasion you are celebrating, there is bound to be a perfect theme that will undoubtedly take your party to the next level. Even if you are not a professional party planner, learning how to choose a theme for your party does not have to be a stressful matter as long as you take the time to consider the occasion, the budget and the people involved.

How to Plan a Surprise Party

Learning how to plan a surprise party is not as difficult as it seems. To achieve the desired effect for these types of parties you would plan the event the same way you would any other celebration, there are just a few additional details you will need to prepare for so that your surprise goes off without a hitch!

Setting a Date

The first important factor when figuring out how to plan a surprise party is to set a definite date and time. You're going to want to set a date that is both good for you and the majority of those on the invite list so ask around before making your decision. Remember, it's not much of a surprise party if no one shows up. You will also want to check with your guest of honor and very casually asked him what kind of plans he has coming up so that you don't plan the party for a time when they are unavailable.

Making the Guest List

Unfortunately, making a guest list can be one of the more difficult aspects of learning how to plan a surprise party. As you are planning a party for someone other than yourself, you will need to do a little digging to make sure that you invite friends from not only your mutual circle but also from circles that that person may otherwise be involved in. Is this person a member of an athletic team or volunteer group? Remember to invite people that this person would invite to their own party so that no one gets left out of the celebration.

Keeping the Secret

It's hard figuring out how to plan a surprise party on your own and at some point you will need help. You will also need the cooperation of all the guests to keep your surprise party a secret. The best way to do this is to tell everyone up front that it is a surprise party. Ask them to keep the secret and not tell the guest of honor, no matter what.

You should also avoid telling any details to those whom you think might be a risk. If your guest of honor has close friends that you worry may tell him but you think they might show up even on short notice, delay telling them until a few days before to give them less time to spill the beans.

Be careful not to leave any written party plans, lists or decorations laying around the house to prevent having to come up with major lies that you may or may not be able to keep track of. Remember, the less you have to lie, the easier it is to keep your secret.

Getting Your Guest of Honor to the Party

Getting your guest of honor to your designated location is most often the hardest part of figuring out how to throw a surprise party. The easiest way to accomplish this is to have several of the guests friends twist the truth and 'make plans' with the guest of honor. If they believe they have solid plans for the evening and everyone shows up on time, it will keep them from getting suspicious. Have the friends get in the car and start driving to their 'originally' planned location.

At that point one of the friends should have an 'emergency' and have to stop by their house or they need to stop somewhere on the way to speak to someone. On the way, text the party coordinator at the party location and give them at least a ten minute warning of your arrival so that they can turn the lights off and hide. You can then proceed to relocate to the party destination.

Surprise!

Once the guest of honor arrives at the house, don't drop the ball by suggesting they open the door. Allow the person who 'had the emergency' open the door and turn on the light. To avoid premature chaos, inform all of the guests to wait until the lights turn on before yelling, "Surprise!"

Learning how to plan a surprise party is not that difficult and you can pull it off quite easily as long as you are working with people whom you can trust to keep your secret. Let people know how important the event is and get them involved. The more excited your team is the easier it will be for them to keep the surprise party a secret.

Create Birthday Party Decorations Cheaply

Planning a birthday party or any theme party for the matter doesn't have to cost a lot of money. Coming up with some fun but cheap ideas will help you stick to a budget.

Shop Wisely

Your local dollar stores or even discount chain stores often have lower prices on party supplies. Many places online if you plan ahead can provide you with many different themes and party supplies. Two of my favorite are Birthday in a Box and Birthday Express. You can shop sales and use reward or coupon websites such as ebates that will give you a rebate back for what you spent. Using these combinations to buy supplies is one of my favorite ways to shop for anything online.

Table Decor

Most parties have at least one main table with a pretty tablecloth, paper plates, napkins, cups, and silverware. You may also have a few extra tables for eating, maybe one for the cake, and one for gifts. White tablecloths are usually cheaper than the colored ones and you can use accents or other decorations to offset the white tablecloth. For a kids party you can even use white butcher paper and arrange cups of crayons, stickers, or other craft supplies around the tables and let each child draw and color to their heart's content.

You don't have to buy cute decorated cups or napkins either. You can save money by buying white and decorating with theme stickers or if you are really crafty you can print designs off the internet. Search the dollar store for big bags of confetti, tissue paper, or even Easter basket grass to spread around to create centerpieces or crazy place settings. Think beyond matching cups and plates and it will cost less and be a lot more creative.

Party Decor

You can easily create your own party hats out of cardstock For a kids party have them make their own noise makers or shakers out of toilet paper rolls and beans or uncooked pasta shells. Tape the ends with paper and have them decorate with markers or stickers. You can also make your own party crackers using toilet paper rolls. Fill each roll with goodies and candies and wrap each twisting the ends with ribbon. Decorate the table with these and each guests can take one how.

Any goodie bags displayed on a table make great decorations and a take home present for the end.

Banners and Hanging Decorations

Banners will last for years if taken care of. They are also simple to make either printing one online or in a large font in a Word document. A sheet of poster board with Happy Birthday written in a coat of glitter paint, or spread on some glue, then sprinkle glitter or confetti over it.

A fun project to do with your child before the party would be to make some hanging lanterns to use as decorations. Glow sticks make a fun effect for a nighttime party.

If you are using a theme for your party, print out images that fit your theme. Attach these items on crepe-paper streamers or on plain old strings with tape, glue, or staples, then hang them from the ceiling, walls, doorways, and windows.

Decorating the Cake

If you make your own cake it can save you money as well. A sheet cake decorated with figurines or candles is for a kids party. Cupcakes are another fun idea that works for a kids or adult party. Display them in a fun way and you don't need an elaborate cake.

Visit learn cake decorating for many easy cake decorating ideas and patterns.

Decorating the Outdoors

A fun idea for parties is always to have balloons outside the house. This not only serves for a fun atmosphere this helps those who don't know where you live to find your house easier.

Go ahead and carry your birthday party theme outside. If your party has a beach theme, for instance, some beach balls or other beach toys at the front door would be fun. Music playing at the front door as your guests arrive is another form of 'decoration' that helps get guests in the party mood.

Ideas for Making Your Own Party Invitations

Once you have decided on a theme there are many ideas for making your own party invitations that can be as simple or as intricate as you want. Invitations for parties created by children, teens and adults give a special flavor to any event.

Invitations for Youngsters

Party invitation ideas for youngsters can include painting hand or foot prints on the front of a folded piece of paper. Choosing ideas with a few steps will be easier for young children to follow while allowing them to explore their own creativity. Stickers, colored adhesive tape and stencils are a few of the ways children can help decorate their own party invitations.

Themed children's party invitations are available from a number of online sources including nickjr.com where Dora the Explorer, Bubble Guppies, Blue's Clues and Umizoomi invitations can be printed at home using your own printer. Thomas the Train, Bob the Builder and many more free party invitations that you can personalize are available by using an online search engine.

Invitations for Older Children

Older children can include party information written by them using colorful markers, glitter glue or ink pens. Themed party invitations are available free online, to be printed, and then colored by the young host with the party information already included. Cutting out shapes from colored paper or using leaves, flower petals or seeds to decorate the outside of a party invitation are additional ideas for making your own party invitations.

Themed parties, especially holiday parties provide a variety of handmade, personalized invitation options. Advent calendar type windows that expose party information when opened and scratch off invitations that use permanent markers with the date and time information hiding under a layer of multi-colored crayon or jigsaw puzzles are fun to make. Invitations that require the recipient to first assemble the puzzle before reading the details are an additional idea for unique party invitations.

Invitations for Teenagers
Creativity combined with the abundance of specialty papers allow teenagers to customize party invitations that will let them express themselves while being creative. Metallic and self-adhesive papers can be cut into shapes, used as borders around photographs or punched into shapes and added to the inside of an invitation. Specialty papers and hole punchers may be purchased at hobby and craft stores as well as online.

Consider making your own paper when creating party invitations as small quantities of homemade paper provide an artistic medium that is unique. Flower petals, seeds, and color are just a few of the many ways to incorporate a wide range of materials into the invitation paper. With a few items and some time making your own special invitation paper is one of many creative ideas that allow you to personalize your party.

A little creativity provides a wide range of ideas for making your own party invitations and most of the materials needed are already on hand.

Outdoor Party Games

Outdoor party games allow guests to romp, play, and be loud, while keeping party clean up to a minimum. Unlike games played indoors, outdoor games let guests be as rambunctious and noisy as they like without worrying about delicate and breakable items.

Sidewalk Chalk Games

Sidewalk chalk is a great way to create a variety of games for younger children including toddlers. Using chalk mark a variety of shapes in different colors on the sidewalk or driveway and make small cards with the same color and shape marked on them. Guests draw a card and find that shape. You can modify this party game for older children by adding music and playing the game like musical chairs. Allowing all guests to play together eliminates the problems that sometimes occur when there is a single winner.

Older children and teens can use colored sidewalk chalk to create murals and art. Instead of allowing all partygoers to draw at the same time, choose two or three guests and set a time limit. Using a kitchen timer, the artists change when the timer goes off. Checkers utilizing guests as markers can be played using a huge chalk checkerboard This is a great outdoor party games for magical or Harry Potter themed parties for older children.

Water Games

Water is always a fun medium for outdoor party games and can be easy for young and old alike. Water balloon transfers let guests try to pass off a small water filled balloon to their partner without using their hands. Water balloon spoon and cup races allow more guests to participate. Fishing for prizes using plastic nets is another interesting game that is easy for all ages. Place small plastic toys or waterproof items in a large container allowing guests to fish for a prize.

Traditional Games

Some games to play outdoors could include:

"**Mother May I**" where one guest standing at the finish line asks another to jump, take steps or hop, however if the person asked does not ask "Mother May I" then they must return to the start of the line.

Red light Green light is another game where one guest says "Green Light" allowing the others to move forward and "Red Light" to stop. The speaker can choose how the others move forward including heel to toe steps, hops or regular steps.

Freeze Tag is played with music allowing guests to run, hop or dance until the music stops. Any guest who moves after the music stops or the person who is in charge says Stop leaves the group.

Children of all ages enjoy being active and outdoor party games gives them the chance to be loud, messy and moving about.

Children Party Game Ideas

Wondering how to entertain the kids coming to your child's party? Children party game ideas abound. Choose age appropriate games with simple contests for children six and under and fun games with a challenge for the older kids. Game supplies can often be improvised from items already in your home such as balls, buckets, socks or squirt guns. Some games may require you to purchase some inexpensive items, but most have other uses around the house.

Simple Games

Children party game ideas should include easy games for the smaller children.

"**Gone Fishing**" is a fun game in which every child wins something. All you need is a blue sheet or shower curtain, some fish appliqués or cutouts, string, a pole and clothes pins. It also helps to have a second adult to assist you. Tie the string about four feet high between two objects and drape the blue sheet over it. Put the fish cutouts on the sheet to resemble water with fish swimming in it.

Tie a string with a clothespin on the end to a pole. Each child goes fishing over the top of the sheet and quickly catches a prize when the other adult, hiding on the other side of the sheet, attaches a bag with candy or small toys to the clothespin and tugs on the line. Some other simple games for younger kids can include:

Cat Tails – Attach strips of cloth to the back of the children's pants making certain they are long enough to drag on the floor. The object of the game is to step on someone else's tail and make it come off while keeping your own in place. The winner is the last one who retains his tail.

Blindfolded Shoe Shuffle – Each child is blindfolded, removes his shoes, and throws them in a pile. An adult mixes them and says "go". The first kid to find his shoes by touch is the winner.

Duck Duck Squirt – Chose someone to be "it", give him a squirt gun, and form the rest of the kids in a circle. That child then goes round the circle and says "duck, duck, squirt" and squirts another child who then chases the squirter back to his place in the circle. If the squirter makes it without being tagged by the other child, he gets to squirt again. This is an excellent option for pool parties and outdoor celebrations.

It is a smart idea with these **children party game ideas** to alternate high energy games with quieter games to keep the festivities from getting out of hand and overtiring the kids.

Games for Older Children

Older kids will prefer more of a challenge so keep that in mind when mulling over your children party game ideas. "Around the Ping Pong Table" requires some dexterity, teamwork, and a ping-pong table. Suitable for up to 15 kids, start the game with two people at each end of the table with paddles and a ball. After one hits the ball he lays down the paddle and another kid takes his place to return the volley. Keep the kids moving clockwise and if a child misses the ball he is out. Some other party game ideas for older kids may include:

Shaving the Balloon – Blow up several balloons and coat them with shaving cream to use this children party game ideas. Give the children plastic knives with which they are to shave their balloon without popping it. The first one to complete the task wins.

Twenty Questions – Write topics such as movies, songs, or famous persons on pieces of paper. The person chosen as "it" knows the topic and can only answer "yes" or "no" to the questions of the children trying to guess the topic. The first child to guess the correct topic wins the prize.

Egg Toss – Outdoor party games can be messy and this one is no exception. Pair off the kids and give each pair an egg. The couples start out about five feet apart and toss the egg to one another. After each successful toss the pairs move further away from each other. The last pair standing with an unbroken egg wins the game.

These **children party game ideas** are simple, inexpensive, and a lot of fun. Adults can also participate and enjoy the games meant for older children, just make sure it is adults playing against other adults.

Some games are better suited to an outdoor venue and some may be more seasonal than others but all of them are designed to elicit squeals of laughter from the kids. If they are really enjoying one game, don't cut it short. Let them play as long as they are having fun.

Fun Kids Birthday Party Games Done Cheaply

Having planned activities and games at parties is one of the keys to a successful party. For grownups, they often are content talking and mingling but adults will even enjoy a few games thrown in here and there. For a kids party, you want a planned itinerary to help the guests not get bored and decide to make their own fun. (Which sometimes could veer off where you'd like the party NOT to go.)

Balloon Fun

The old fashion sticking candies and trinkets inside balloons, blowing them up and displaying them on a sheet of wood can still be a favorite. Using darts to pop the balloons works best but allow a safety zone for this activity.

During summer months, a water balloon toss is a perfect fun activity that never grows old.

Pin-the-Tail Games

How about a "Pin the Tail on the Donkey" or any variation of it. For kids 6-10 years old but you can make this game harder or more themed for different events.
You can print off pictures online that fit your theme party and come up with ideas like Pin Crown on the Princess or "Pin the Antenna on the Alien" or whatever your child likes.

Pick a Duck

Find rubber ducks or other floating toys at your dollar store. They are usually sold in packages rather cheaply. Write a number on each duck and place in a big bucket or child's pool full of water. Each guest picks a duck and will receive the corresponding goodies with the number on it.

This same idea can be used with fish and you can create your own fishing pond. You can make it more challenging by making a fishing pole out of a stick and string.

Attaching a magnet to the end of your pole and one magnet to each duck or fish they need to "catch" a fish. Alternately you can make a loop at the end of your pole with string and they have to scoop the fish or duck into the loop.

Musical Dress Up

Musical chairs is always a fun game but another variation is to use old clothes, shoes, hats, scarves, jewelry, whatever odds and ends you can gather together cheaply or borrow.

The idea of the game is while the music is playing each guest must dress up as fast and funny as they can before the music stops.

Have a judge give out awards with funny names like "Most Silly", "Most Colorful", etc

Teenage Party Games

Organizing some teenage party games for your teenagers to play at their party will be a great way for them to have fun and to help you worry less about what they're doing. You can have games, which you organize and run, or games where you provide the resources and the group goes off and plays by themselves.

Getting this balance right is key for the success of your teenager's party, as they will find it hard to forgive you if you do something they think isn't cool. Your best bet is to run your games past them first and get their opinions and ideas as well.

Adult-Led Fun

Choosing the right teenage party games will depend on the attitude of your teenager towards games, but some activities will engage even the surliest of teenagers. Try organizing

Flashlight tag – Wait until it is good and dark outside, then choose one person to be "It" and give them a flashlight. Get the others to go out into the yard and hide. When "It" comes out, the other players must start to run from hiding place to hiding place. "It" shines his or her light around the yard, and anyone who gets caught in the beam becomes "It". You can play last man standing where tagged players are out and must sit aside until the next game.

Scavenger hunt – Is one of the best teenage party games for older kids as it allows them the freedom to explore under certain guidelines. Give each group a camera and a list of tasks to perform around the neighborhood such as "take a photo of someone on a skateboard" or "take a photo of someone on your team doing a handstand".

Give them a time limit and award prizes for the first
team back and the best photos.

Truth or dare – This is a borderline game to play, but if
you're in charge of the game, you can avoid silly dares
or embarrassing questions. You could spend some time
with your teen before the party devising the questions
and preparing elaborate dares, some of which will be
more exciting than others as they won't have to be
hidden from adult view.

Board Games

Your teenager might not appreciate having adult input into
their party, so it will be useful to have some independent
teenage party games that you have provided as a way for
them to have fun safely, but away from your supervision:

Twister – The party classic needs no introduction, but
allows your teen guests to get a little bit closer to each
other in an appropriate way.

Pictionary – A great team game where participants have to
draw clues to words given to them. A quick-thinking
game that takes a few minutes to explain, they'll
happily play it for hours.

Apples to Apples – A fairly new arrival to the party game
scene, but one that you can play with the family as well
as with friends. Each player gets a hand full of cards
with nouns on, such as people, places or objects. One
player turns over an adjective card and each person has
to choose the best matching noun from their hand. One
player acts as judge and chooses the match they like
best. This quick game usually results in gales of
laughter.

The most important thing to remember when planning
teenage party games is that your guests will strive to look

cool in front of their peers, so you'll need to make sure that you're not asking them to do something they'll consider babyish or something embarrassing.

Adult Party Games

Games are not just for kids; try some adult party games at your next soiree. Until your guests get into the flow of the party they may feel a little awkward. Whether you are having a singles party or one for couples, a dinner party, or just an informal mingling of friends, a game can make people relax, interact, and have a good time.

Games should be selected to suit the occasion. For example, if most of the attendees are single and especially if they don't know each other very well, the party will get a jump start with an ice breaker game. Couples might enjoy games that test how well they know each other. For a younger crowd the games might be a bit more physical and adult party games for a dinner party will need to be of a fashion that won't disrupt the meal and the stream of conversation.

Lie Detector Game

A great game to use as an icebreaker, this game can be played by friends or at a party that includes people not well known to each other. On the invitation, or at least prior to the party, instruct each guest to write down three statements about themselves. Two of the statements should be true but one should be a believable falsehood. To begin the party, have each guest recite their statements. The other guests then try to determine which statement is the lie. In the course of the game players will invariably give more information about themselves and your guests will interact and become better acquainted.

Hula Hoop Games

Any number of adult party games can be devised using the simple hula hoop that we mastered as children but, as adults, its intricacies baffle us. You could simply see who can keep hula hooping the longest or determine who can complete the most hoops in 10 seconds. If you have the space, see who can roll a hoop the farthest. Along those same lines, stage a hula hoop ring toss game using guests as the targets. Since motion breeds emotion this is also a good type of game to get the party rolling.

Newlywed Game

Adult party games for couples can be the most fun. Just like the television show, the newlywed game will pit the guys against the gals. Determine which couples want to play and write your list of questions and a bonus question. Keep a four couple limit per game and let the other guests serve as the panel of judges and scorekeepers. Some questions eliciting funny answers might include:

> What is your spouse's most grating habit
> Who was your spouse's first/last boy or girlfriend
> If shipwrecked on an island what is the one thing your spouse would miss the most
> If your spouse won the lottery what would he or she do with the money

It is best if you choose questions that will keep the game good-natured and not start a family fight.

Message Under the Plate

Adult party games can stimulate conversation at dinner parties. Message under the plate is an easy game to play. On several small pieces of paper write several different odd but usable phrases and place one under each plate. Each attendee is instructed to read their phrase but not share it with anyone else. The object of the game is to conversationally use the phrase during the dinner and see if anyone else detects that it is the odd phrase.

Enjoyment is the key to a successful party and adult party games will make your guests interact, laugh at each other, and laugh at themselves.

Live Entertainment done Cheaply

Having live events such as a professional singer or rock band isn't practical unless you have one in the family. Magic shows and clown acts are fun but not everyone likes them.

Make your own Musical Fun

Use a stereo or ipod speakers and create a list of songs guests can sing. Print off the lyrics off the internet. You can include prizes for the best singers or other awards.

For younger kids, have them make musical instruments out of paper plates, paper towel tubes, bells, whistles, or whatever makes a fun sound. Then let the kids create their own music and lyrics to go along.

Puppet Playhouse Fun

Using a large box you can create your own theater. Using paint, fabric, stickers, glitter, and other embellishments, you can decorate it anyway you would like. Then decide on your puppets. If you are handy at sewing, look for patterns online for simple people or animal puppets to make using a variety of materials, including fabric, felt, yarn, and even old socks.

For a craft project kids can make their own puppets using brown paper bags and craft materials. They can create characters and the story to tell during the puppet show. You could choose to use small paper bags and create hand puppets, or use large paper bags and the kids can actually become the puppet. Then these 'kid size' puppets would come out and act out the play as their character.

Silly Story in the Round Fun

Telling a story in a circle can provide some fun story lines. One person starts the story by choosing a beginning line out of a hat. Prepare some story beginnings beforehand on sheets of paper. Ideas could be Once there was a boy who didn't like his dinner or In a far away land there lived a little rabbit. Whatever ideas you can come up with to start a story off. After the first person reads the line the next person has to add more to the story.

The object is for the story to get sillier and more involved, picking up more characters with each new storyteller. Make sure each guest gets a turn starting and ending the story.

Think beyond video games and movies and your party can be a lot of fun!

Kids Party Crafts or Activities

Entertaining children does not have to be difficult especially if you provide kids party crafts or activities that give them something to do. Kids are full of energy and finding activities or crafts that will interest them while letting them be creative are the answer to most parties.

Toddlers and Young Children

Toddlers are curious and tend to explore their world through touch, sight and taste. Using homemade edible paint, painters drop cloths and butcher paper, allows young partygoers to paint a party picture and then to take it home.

By mixing dry pudding mix or corn syrup with food coloring added, little ones can paint and taste without any need for concern. Adding texture to the edible paint using cornmeal combines sculpture with painting.

Sticker Crafts and Cake Decorating

Stickers provide many kids party crafts or activities for all ages, even toddlers. Foam shaped stickers, eye, mouth and nose stickers and even hand cut stickers created from adhesive backed specialty paper can be used to decorate pumpkins, apples and Styrofoam balls, cones and boxes.

Allowing young party goers to decorate their own iced cupcake is a great way to entertain and provide a safe, edible activity. Muffin tins filled with a variety of sprinkles, cake decorations and non-perils let guests choose what they want on their cake.

Paper Crafts

Paper plates are very crafty especially when it comes to

kids party activities. Older children can create mosaics using colored, metallic or textured paper while younger children can make animals, birds, insects and other interesting shapes using paper plates.

Transform water and soda bottles into musical instruments by covering in decorated paper and dropping small beans or pebbles inside. Adult supervision is required for younger children who may put pebbles, pasta, beans or seeds into their mouths.

Older children can use prepared metal lids to create cymbals, tambourines, castanets and shakers using metal washers, large buttons, metal bells and smaller lids. Instructions for crafts can be found at your local library or online.

Paper towel and toilet paper tubes are great for kids party crafts or activities as they can be used to make rain sticks, handkerchief parachutes that can be tossed into the air, or decorated canisters to hold special trinkets.

Scavenger Hunts
Scavenger hunts are fun activities in which toddlers can also participate by using cards with images instead of a written list of things to find. The older the party guest the more involved the hunt can be especially if the scavengers are playing outside.

Small parties can have individual lists of items to find and providing items that they can take home only increases the fun. Larger parties may want to have small groups search for items on their list and awarding handmade ribbons to all participants. We have a scavenger hunt list on the following page.

Kids party crafts or activities that include creativity and fun are the best things to offer regardless of what is being celebrated.

Outdoor Scavenger Hunt List
Be careful what you touch and pick up from the outdoors!

Collect one of each:

- **Flower**
- **Leaf**
- **Something red**
- **Find something soft**
- **Feather**
- **Acorn or other nut**
- **Small rock that fits in the palm of your hand**
- **A pinecone**
- **Small stick as long as your hand**
- **A piece of garbage that needs to be thrown away**

Tips for a Perfect Baked Cake

These tips for a perfect baked cake are designed to be general principles that can be applied to a cake for any occasion, whether you want a simple banana cake or a fancy layered desert cake. While a true baker knows every cake is different, there are tips you can always follow to help make sure your creation comes out of the oven just right.

Tip #1: Preparation

Many a beautiful kitchen creation has been spoiled by poor preparation. Always ensure you have the ingredients you need, in the right quantities, before you even begin. There's nothing more frustrating to a cake baker than getting half way through the recipe and finding you don't have enough eggs. Clean and arrange the kitchen so that everything is at hand when you need it.

Tip #2: The Pan

An important but often overlooked aspect of baking a perfect cake. The shape and size of the pan can play a big part in the outcome of the finished product, regardless of how well you do everything else. As well as following the recipe's instructions for preparing the pan, you should take into account factors like the size and thickness as these can have an effect on how long the cake should be baked for and the oven temperature. Also, if the pan is too small and the mixture is close to spilling over the edges, this can ruin the shape of the cake as it begins to rise and expand.

Also be aware that an old pan blackened by use will absorb more heat and bake faster, whereas a shiny new pan reflects more heat, thus slowing down the baking process. This is why you can follow a recipe to the letter and still end up with a burnt cake if you're using a beaten up old pan.

Tip #3: Understanding the Science of Cake

Don't worry, we're not about to get too technical here. What this tip refers to mostly is you understand of how a cake takes shape and how the ingredients combine to make the final creation. For instance, it helps to understand the leavening agents in your cake - the ingredients that make it rise when you put it in the oven.

The leavening agent will depend on the type of the cake you're making and the recipe you use, but it will typically be baking soda, baking powder, air or occasionally yeast - or some combination of these. You should know what the leavening agent is, because if for example the leavening agent is air this will make a difference to how thoroughly you stir and mix the ingredients before baking.

Tip #4: Removing the Cake

The last of our tips for a perfect baked cake deals with making sure it stays in one piece (until you're ready to eat it, that is). This is the point where many an otherwise-perfect cake has come to grief. Timing can play a factor in this, but there are a few things you can do to help ease the cake out without running into trouble. One is to tap the pan lightly on the counter to remove air pockets before you remove the cake. Another is to simply insert a greased lining into the pan before you pour in the mix or grease your pan well and then simply remove the lining with the cake.

Cake Decorating Design Ideas

Simple Cake Decorating Ideas

A common way to decorate a cake is to add small flowers made of colored gel to the edges by using a standard petal tip on the end of the icing bag.

One idea requires the use of only one tip, white butter cream icing, a flower cookie cutter and different gel colors. Simply put the butter cream icing on the cake, let it dry, and then gently press the flower cookie cutter into the icing. Use the gel to outline the flowers and different color creams to fill the insides as well as the yellow center. Add a few green lines for stems and leaves and you have a cake covered in pretty flowers.

If you feel up to doing something a little more difficult, you might try making flowers with fondant and sticking them on top of the butter cream or around the sides of the cake. Other decorative cake ideas that are easy to make are bears, Elmo, a cross, or a house with the use of shaped cake pans and colorful icing.

Ornate Cake Decorating

Cake decorating design ideas with underwater themes are highly decorative, and might be easy or slightly challenging to create depending on your patience and culinary skills. To make a cake adorned with fish and coral, you first need to roll out white and light blue fondant, knead them together to create a marbleized look, and place it over the butter cream onto the cake. Next, melt some white candy and put it into the icing bag so that you can squeeze it out into coral shapes. Sprinkle nonpareils on top of the shapes and let them harden in the refrigerator before placing them around the sides of the cake.

Finally, form tropical fish by adding food color to the butter in the rice krispy treats recipe. Roll the rice cereal into a ball and mold fruit snacks and gum drops into the shapes of tails, fins, mouth and eyes. Sit the fish on top of the cake and it's ready to serve. Princess castles, baby carriages, cathedral Bundt cakes, and seashells are a few more ideas that you can nicely decorate.

Elaborate Cake Decorating

For the advanced culinary artist or those who don't mind trying new things, there are many elaborate cake decorating design ideas, such as a three-dimensional wedding dress, penguin, hamburger or jungle scene. Dinosaurs, jack-o-lanterns, and sports cakes also make for very detailed and challenging arrangements but the end result is a design that is sure to have guests talking.

Of these over-the-top designs, the sports cakes are the easiest to construct. For example, the golf cake is only two layers of cake placed on top of each other and covered with chocolate icing and cookie crumbs. Then you just melt some green candies and spread the paste onto wax paper so that a long, thick strip is created. Let the candy harden for about a half hour until you cut it into smaller pieces of various sizes. Place the "grass" on top of and around the cake, add a real golf ball or make an edible one and you're done.

Party Food Ideas

Coming up with good party food ideas is essential to having a successful party and catering to guests of different ages is sometimes difficult. Children are often picky, teens are almost always watching their weight, and some adults have dietary restrictions, so pleasing everyone, especially while trying to stay within a budget, might seem like a challenge. However, if you plan ahead and do some reading, making the food could be your easiest task.

Keeping it Simple

Cheese and crackers are traditional but versatile and you get a lot for your money, especially if you add a few tomato slices, olives, pepperoni, or other Italian cold cut meat. By adding to this common platter, you are giving guests more choices and pleasing more palettes

On another platter, you might offer fresh vegetables with a dip or if you prefer to serve something a little healthier, opt for hummus, which guests can also spread on their cheese and crackers

These simple, affordable snacks complement each other, increasing options, and offer something for the vegan, the meat eater, the weight watcher, and the fussy eater. This is what you must keep in mind, as options are the key when serving food to a variety of guests.

BBQ Basics

Summertime is party time and just about everyone loves a good cookout, but there are a few party food ideas to make your BBQ stand out from the rest.

Instead of serving the usual hamburger, serve inside out burgers and set up a condiment bar that offers feta cheese, cucumber sauce, and chopped olives for a taste of the

Mediterranean

You might also decide to offer guests pitas instead of hamburger rolls, since they are less messy and lower in calories

For a side dish, potato salad is quite popular, but tangy potato salad with paprika and a hint of jalapeno is one way to make it interesting.

Substitute sweet potato fries for ordinary fries.

Pulled pork, ribs or hot dogs is another fun party food.

A Fancy Tea Party
Finger sandwiches, fresh baked scones, a box full of herbal and fruit-inspired tea bags, and maybe some yogurt parfaits with fresh fruit are perfect party food ideas when you want to entertain family and friends over tea. Shrimp cocktail and some hors d'oeuvres, while not common at a tea party, offer variety and add a touch of elegance to your event. Petit fours or other miniature deserts, uncommon on a daily basis, add the finishing touch to this exquisite event.

Just for Kids
Pizza is generally a big hit among kids, so making mini-pizzas, or "pizzettes," is one of the smart and modern party food ideas that cater to children. By making small pizzas, you avoid waste, increase the variety of topping choices, and don't have to cut anything.

Mini-burgers, or sliders, are another great finger food for kids, along with pigs in a blanket and grilled cheese. Unfortunately, these are not healthy foods for kids to eat, so substituting whole wheat bread, turkey hot dogs, or low fat cheese will fill bellies the healthy way and keep parents happy at the same time.

Are You Ready for Some Football?
Party food ideas are easy when it comes time for the Superbowl, since all you need are chicken wings, hot sauce, and foot long sandwiches. To spice things up a bit, you might also choose to serve a seven-layer taco dip, warm bowls of chili, quesadillas, or nachos. To complete this high calorie feast, serve cupcakes and some fresh baked cookies instead of cake or pie.

Whatever event you are planning, a little creativity in the menu will have your guests talking about your party for a long time.

Children's Birthday Party Food

Children's birthday party food should be simple to prepare and easy to eat. Your budget, the location of the party and the age of the children will be a huge factor in determining which foods you will serve. In most cases, you will also find that because there is so much to do the day of the party, any food that can be prepared the day before and refrigerated overnight you should certainly bump to the top of the list.

Children like colorful foods and if you are able to, cutting the snacks into unique shapes is even better. Also, take into consideration the age of the guests. Since most kids can turn any food into finger food, go with the flow. Don't forget to have plenty of napkins and wet wipes.

The Cake

The cake and ice cream are must haves when it comes to children's birthday party food. The cake can be a standard two or three layer round, or single-layer rectangular sheet cake, which has plenty of room for decorations. Also, a theme cake baked in the shape of a cartoon character or that is thematically decorated will be photo-worthy. While you want the cake to be special, you don't have to decorate it as elaborately as a wedding cake. Children will admire it more with their taste buds than their eyes.

The Menu

Sandwiches are often a staple children's birthday party food. Let your creativity shine and cut the bread into shapes with cookie cutters before building the sandwich. For an easily prepared yet creative finger-food, try making sandwich wheels. After removing the crust from whole wheat bread, roll out the slices with a rolling pin. Spread on cream cheese and insert a piece of celery before rolling it up.

Jell-O boats are another colorful and easy to make party food. Halve a few oranges and scoop out the flesh. Mix several flavors of Jell-O and pour into the empty oranges. When the Jell-O has set, cut the halves into fourths and arrange them on a serving tray. In the same sentiment, rainbow cups are also a big hit with kids. Get small clear plastic cups, and one color at a time, pour different colors of Jell-O into them. Be sure to let each layer gel before adding the next layer.

Children's birthday party food can also be healthy:

Prepare zucchini cheesecake the day before the party and warm it in a microwave before serving.

Make an easy fruit boat by scooping the flesh out of the ends of a watermelon with a melon baller and then using the ends as shells into which you can put the watermelon balls, cantaloupe, strawberries and grapes. If you have a little talent and a template, cut the melon to resemble the open mouth of a shark.

Frozen bananas are easy. Make by inserting popsicle sticks into bananas and then rolling them in honey before coating them with coconut. Put them in the freezer overnight and they will be ready for the next day's party.

Quick Treats
 If you're short on time and need quick party food ideas, don't forget to consider these traditional snacks:
mini pizzas
Popcorn

Hot dogs
Cocktail sausages in barbecue sauce
Strawberries dipped in chocolate
Cheese tray
deli meat platters
deviled eggs
hot dog rollups
mini corndogs
vegetable platters
fruit platters

Tips

At birthday parties, kids are hit-and-run eaters. Older kids might sit down to eat, but the younger kids will be playing food-in-hand. Don't forget to ask parents about any food allergies or lactose intolerance issues.

Plan and prepare the children's birthday party food as much as possible the day before the party. Also, keep the birthday cake out of sight until you are ready to serve it. Birthdays are a time to gratify the sweet tooth but it is best not to turn it into sugar-fest. If you are having cake and ice cream try not to include cookies in the menu as well.

See more kids cooking ideas at http://www.kids-cooking-activities.com

Party Favor Ideas and Goody Bags

It does not have to be a challenge to come up with party favor ideas and goody bags. Not only can you match them to your theme, but you can make them age appropriate, or opt for healthy snacks instead of candy and inexpensive trinkets.

Party guests, depending on their age, can make their own favors or fill their own goody bags, ensuring they like everything they take home. You also have the option of keeping things simple and traditional, though adding a little something extra is always a positive gesture.

Babies and Toddlers

Obviously, you can't give most favors or goodies to babies and there are limits as to what you can offer to toddlers, but a general rule of thumb is never give them anything small or hard, like bouncy balls and sucker candy. If you are having a party for a baby but the guests are not babies, chocolate molded lollipops, or chocolate covered fruit if you want to be healthy, are great favors. If you want to avoid food, give guests a small picture frame or a seedling kit to plant a tree in their yard or community garden.

Party favor ideas and goody bags for toddlers usually incorporate the theme of the party. For instance, a Dora the Explorer party might consist of a small Dora plush doll, Dora stickers, and a miniature coloring book or note pad featuring the popular cartoon character.

This traditional idea still works and most people don't expect anything different, but if you have guests that are hard to please, you could throw in some play-doh, modeling clay, a kaleidoscope, or small storybooks. These items are all useful, fun, and age appropriate, ensuring that they won't end up in the trash.

Between Toddlers and Tweens

As kids start getting older, party favor ideas and goody bags become more difficult to figure out since boys and girls like different things. To resolve this problem, either fill the goody bags with all neutral items or make separate bags for the boys and the girls. Older children usually prefer candy to trinkets anyway but you can substitute with fun, healthy snacks, such as fruit snacks, popcorn, or parfaits.

If you opt for trinkets, you might fill goody bags for girls with fake jewelry, a compact mirror, or brush, nail polish, or make up and substitute the plastic goody bag with a small purse or tote. For boys, a goody bag could include Hot Wheels, a small action figure, toy dinosaurs or animals, or gags like a hand buzzer or disappearing ink.

Make the goodies a part of the fun by including them in the party fun. For example, if the party is a summertime event with a focus on water fun, include water squirters, pool toys they can use during the party and take home with them.

Craft Projects, painting wooden items or painting on a blank canvas make excellent party activities. T-shirts, headbands, barrettes, hats, bracelets, necklaces, and other apparel are great items you can decorate with embellishments as well. Decorated aprons for a kids cooking party are always fun. All of these items are something kids can take their finished product home with them.

Teens

This is an even more difficult age group to please, as they

often want everything yet they have everything. It is difficult to come up with party favor ideas and goody bags are no longer an option.

Buy blank cds and let teens create their own music cds with their favorite songs.

Party favors for young ladies might include a scrapbook or a small, inexpensive jewelry box. They will also enjoy an at-home spa-in-a-basket filled with body wash, moisturizing lotion, and loofah or bath gloves.

Favors for teenage boys might include a wallet, a key chain featuring the local sports team or a small bag of homemade cookies. Other party favors for young men may be a voucher for a free movie rental at the neighborhood video store, or an iTunes card so they can download a few songs.

Depending on your budget, and the occasion, you can expand on these ideas and get favors that "wow" your guests. If you are creative and do some research, which is often how the best ideas come to you, coming up with **party favor ideas and goody bags** should be easy. It also helps to consider your guests and don't just buy or make what you want.

How to Sew Goodie Bags for Parties

You will need to sew these goodie bags:
For each bag, two pieces of material cut 9x7 inches.
For the straps, two pieces of material 8 x 2. Or you can use ribbon,1-2 inches wide and 8-9 inches long

Place right sides together on two bag pieces. Sew along three edges leaving the top open. Set aside and sew straps. If using a strip of fabric, 10x3 inches, Fold your long edges into the middle one overlapping slightly the other. Pin in place down the middle. Sew zigzag or straight stitch down the middle enclosing the edges in your seams. Repeat with second strap. If using ribbon you can skip to step 3.
Taking your bag, turn right sides out and fold top edge down 1/4 inch. Add strap or ribbon end to your folded edge and fold down again enclosing strap within the fold. Pin in place. Making sure strap is pointing up. Sew top edge taking out pins as you go.
That's it! Continue process until you have a bag for each party guest and perhaps a few extras.
Stuff with party favors.

You can find this project and more sewing ideas at
http://www.kids-sewing-projects.com

Printed in Great Britain
by Amazon